THIS
BOOK
BELONGS

WATFORD

C000298048

Name: Age:

Favourite player:

2023/24

My Predictions	Actual
The Hornets' final position:	
The Hornets' top scorer:	
Championship winners:	
Championship top scorer:	
FA Cup winners:	
EFL Cup winners:	

Contributors: Peter Rogers, Sam Tighe.

A TWOCAN PUBLICATION

©2023. Published by twocan under licence from Watford Football Club.

978-1-915571-54-0   **£10**

PICTURE CREDITS: Action Images, Alamy, Alan Cozzi and Press Association

WATFORD

CONTENTS

THE CHAMPIONSHIP SQUAD 2023/24

Daniel BACHMANN

1

POSITION: Goalkeeper **COUNTRY:** Austria **DOB:** 09/07/1994

Having topped Watford's appearance ranks last season - missing just one of 46 Championship games - goalkeeper Daniel Bachmann signed a new five-year contract and was appointed Club Captain ahead of the 2023/24 campaign. The Austria international - who was his country's main goalkeeper at Euro 2020 - joined the Hornets in 2017, and played a key role in promotion to the Premier League in 2020/21.

Jeremy NGAKIA

2

POSITION: Defender **COUNTRY:** England **DOB:** 07/09/2000

Signed in the summer of 2020 - following his departure from West Ham United - right-back Jeremy Ngakia made a strong first impression at Watford, scoring in a friendly against Scunthorpe United and then winning the club's Player of the Month award that September. After making 45 appearances in his first two seasons as a Hornet, Ngakia was hampered by injury for much of 2022/23, but he still managed 14 Championship outings.

Francisco
SIERRALTA

3

POSITION: Defender   **COUNTRY:** Chile   **DOB:** 06/05/1997

Chile international defender Francisco Sierralta arrived from Udinese at the start of the 2020/21 campaign a relative unknown among Watford supporters, but made an excellent impression by becoming a regular in a backline that conceded just 30 goals all season en route to promotion. After featuring five times in the Premier League in 2021/22, the former Parma and Empoli man was again more prominent in the second-tier during 2022/23, making 20 appearances in all competitions.

Wesley
HOEDT

4

POSITION: Defender   **COUNTRY:** Netherlands   **DOB:** 06/03/1994

Former Southampton and Anderlecht centre-half Wesley Hoedt has established himself as an important member of Watford's squad following his January 2023 signing, being named in the leadership group ahead of 2023/24. A full Netherlands international - with six caps to his name - Hoedt scored on his debut for the Hornets, in a 1-1 draw at home to Blackburn Rovers a month after his arrival at Vicarage Road.

Ryan
PORTEOUS

5

POSITION: Defender   **COUNTRY:** Scotland   **DOB:** 25/03/1999

Defender Ryan Porteous marked his first Watford appearance with a goal in February 2023's 2-2 draw at Reading, just over a week after swapping Hibernian for Vicarage Road. Born in Dalkeith, and a product of the Hibs academy, he made his senior Scotland bow against Ukraine in September 2022, and finished the 2022/23 season with 17 Hornets outings to his name.

Jamal
LEWIS

6

POSITION: Defender   **COUNTRY:** Northern Ireland   **DOB:** 25/01/1998

Watford confirmed the signing of defender Jamal Lewis in July 2023, on a season-long loan deal from Newcastle United with an option to buy. The Northern Ireland international - who has featured regularly for his country since his March 2018 debut - came through the club ranks at Norwich City, before switching to Newcastle in September 2020 for a reported £15 million fee and going on to make 36 appearances in all competitions for the Magpies.

Tom
INCE
7

POSITION: Forward **COUNTRY:** England **DOB:** 30/01/1992

Experienced forward Tom Ince joined the Golden Boys ahead of the 2023/24 season, having scored 11 goals in 54 appearances for Reading during a year-and-a-half stint. The England youth international - son of former Manchester United and Liverpool midfielder Paul - started his career at Liverpool, and has also enjoyed notable spells at the likes of Blackpool, Derby County and Stoke City. He made his Watford debut against Stoke in August 2023.

Jake
LIVERMORE
8

POSITION: Midfielder **COUNTRY:** England **DOB:** 14/11/1989

Midfielder Jake Livermore penned a one-year deal at Watford in July 2023, following his departure from fellow Championship side West Bromwich Albion. The Enfield native enjoyed seven separate loans while on the books at Tottenham Hotspur until 2014, before signing permanent terms with Hull City and later spending six-and-a-half years at the Hawthorns. Capped seven times by England between 2012 and 2017, Livermore made his Hornets debut against QPR in August 2023.

Mileta
RAJOVIĆ

9

POSITION: Forward   **COUNTRY:** Denmark   **DOB:** 17/07/1999

The Hornets snapped up forward Mileta Rajović from Kalmar FF in August 2023, after he had scored seven goals in the first 10 games of the 2023/24 Swedish season. The Denmark native began his career with Brøndby and Randers, but made a major impact at Næstved Boldklub, scoring 30 goals in 58 matches before moving to Kalmar in December 2022. He made his Watford bow just two days after signing, against Blackburn Rovers.

WATFORD

Imrân
LOUZA
10

POSITION: Midfielder   **COUNTRY:** Morocco   **DOB:** 01/05/1999

Creative midfielder Imrân Louza had spent his whole life in Nantes before Watford came calling in the summer of 2021. The Morocco international - who came through the ranks at the team nicknamed 'The Yellow House' - played 43 times in his first two seasons in England, before being handed the number 10 shirt ahead of 2023/24. He opened his goalscoring account in the current season against QPR on the opening day.

Ismaël
KONÉ
11

POSITION: Midfielder   **COUNTRY:** Canada   **DOB:** 16/06/2002

Canadian midfielder Ismaël Koné joined Watford at the start of the 2023 January transfer window, having featured in each of his nation's group games at the 2022 World Cup. Born in the Ivory Coast before moving to North America aged seven and establishing himself at CF Montréal, Koné went on to feature 16 times in the Championship in the latter half of the 2022/23 campaign.

Ken
SEMA
12

POSITION: Midfielder   **COUNTRY:** Sweden   **DOB:** 30/09/1993

Versatile wideman Ken Sema joined Watford from Östersunds FK in July 2018. The Sweden international - who was included in his country's Euro 2020 squad - spent 2019/20 on loan at Udinese, after helping the Hornets reach the 2019 FA Cup final. He made 41 appearances in the 2020/21 promotion season and was one of the standout stars of 2022/23, notching five goals and eight assists in 40 league games.

Rhys
HEALEY
14

POSITION: Forward   **COUNTRY:** England   **DOB:** 06/12/1994

Forward Rhys Healey signed a two-year deal in Hertfordshire in June 2023 following a three-year spell in France, where he scored 39 times in 77 appearances for Toulouse. The Manchester native began his career in Wales with Connah's Quay Nomads and then Cardiff City, while he has also turned out for the likes of Colchester United and MK Dons. He made his first Watford appearance against Stevenage in the Carabao Cup.

Mattie
POLLOCK
15

POSITION: Defender   **COUNTRY:** England   **DOB:** 28/09/2001

Young centre-half Mattie Pollock joined Watford in May 2021, having impressed in his 58 appearances for League Two outfit Grimsby Town. A successful loan spell in League One with Cheltenham Town yielded 39 games and the club's 2021/22 Young Player of the Season award, while five outings back with the Hornets at the start of last term preceded another productive loan move, this time at Aberdeen where he scored two goals in 15 games.

Giorgi
CHAKVETADZE
16

POSITION: Midfielder   **COUNTRY:** Georgia   **DOB:** 29/08/1999

Exciting attacking midfielder Giorgi Chakvetadze joined Watford on a season-long loan with an option to buy from KAA Gent in August 2023. The Georgia international's career began in his hometown with Dinamo Tbilisi before he moved to Belgium in the summer of 2017, where he struck eight times in 81 games for Gent. Temporary moves to Hamburger SV and Slovan Bratislava preceded his move to the Hornets, who he first represented against QPR on 2023/24 opening day.

Yáser
ASPRILLA
18

POSITION: Midfielder   **COUNTRY:** Colombia   **DOB:** 19/11/2003

Colombian playmaker Yáser Asprilla joined the Hornets from Envigado in his native country in 2022/23 pre-season. He went on to play 37 Championship games last term, scoring his first goal against Huddersfield Town in April 2023. Asprilla is a full international - having made his senior debut in January 2022 - while he was one of the standout stars of the 2023 Under-20 World Cup in Argentina.

Vakoun
BAYO

19

POSITION: Forward **COUNTRY:** Ivory Coast **DOB:** 10/01/1997

Ivorian forward Vakoun Bayo linked up with the Hornets in the summer of 2022, having started his career in Tunisia and impressed at the likes of Celtic, KAA Gent and RSC Charleroi. After scoring four goals in 24 Championship appearances for Watford in the first half of 2022/23 Bayo returned to Charleroi on loan, before netting two in two at the start of 2023/24 back in Hertfordshire.

Tom
DELE-BASHIRU **24**

POSITION: Midfielder **COUNTRY:** Nigeria **DOB:** 17/09/1999

Manchester City youth product Tom Dele-Bashiru joined Watford on a six-year deal in July 2019, going on to score his first goal for the club against Tranmere Rovers in the FA Cup six months later. Injury has interrupted much of his time at Vicarage Road, but after 39 appearances on loan at Reading in 2021/22, and six back with the Hornets last term, he started 2023/24 brightly with a goal just 33 seconds into the campaign.

Ben
HAMER **26**

POSITION: Goalkeeper **COUNTRY:** England **DOB:** 20/11/1987

Experienced glovesman Ben Hamer has primarily served as back-up to Daniel Bachmann since joining the Hornets in July 2022, making his debut against Coventry City towards the end of 2022/23. The former Charlton Athletic, Leicester City and Swansea City stopper - who played in the Champions League for the Foxes - made his first appearance of 2023/24 in August's Carabao Cup defeat at Stevenage.

Matheus
MARTINS
37

POSITION: Forward   **COUNTRY:** Brazil   **DOB:** 16/07/2003

Tricky young forward Matheus Martins re-joined the Hornets on loan from Udinese in July 2023, having also spent the second half of 2022/23 at Vicarage Road. After a first spell that yielded six appearances, the Brazil youth international - who starred at the 2023 Under-20 World Cup in Argentina with two goals in five games - was one of the Hornets' brightest sparks at the start of 2023/24, scoring on the opening day against QPR.

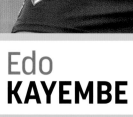

Edo
KAYEMBE
39

POSITION: Midfielder   **COUNTRY:** DR Congo   **DOB:** 03/06/1998

Following spells with Anderlecht and KAS Eupen in Belgium, DR Congo international midfielder Edo Kayembe became a Hornet in January 2022, going on to feature 13 times in the Premier League in the latter half of 2021/22. After starting 2022/23 as a regular feature of the team, injury curtailed his involvement after the World Cup, and he finally made a welcome return to action on the opening day of 2023/24 against QPR.

Myles
ROBERTS
40

POSITION: Goalkeeper   COUNTRY: England   DOB: 09/12/2001

After working his way through the ranks at Reading, young goalkeeper Myles Roberts switched to Watford in January 2020. A string of productive temporary spells in non-league - such as at National League South outfits Concord Rangers in 2021/22 and Welling United in 2022/23 - provided Roberts with valuable experience before he appeared on the Watford first-team bench for the first time against Coventry City in April 2023.

Alfie
MARRIOTT
41

POSITION: Goalkeeper   COUNTRY: England   DOB: 26/03/2004

Watford born and bred, prospective goalkeeper Alfie Marriott joined the Hornets in 2012 and gradually worked his way through the ranks before being handed a squad number ahead of 2023/24. He enjoyed a productive loan spell at non-league Kings Langley during 2021/22 - which saw him make a vital penalty save on the final day of the season - and was part of the Golden Boys' first-team travelling matchday squad on several occasions during 2022/23.

James
MORRIS
42

POSITION: Defender **COUNTRY:** England **DOB:** 23/11/2001

Left-back James Morris has established himself as a key member of the first-team squad, having initially earned a contract in the summer of 2021 after impressing on trial. The former Southampton man made his professional debut against Leicester City in the FA Cup in January 2022, before featuring in 12 Championship games in 2022/23. He started 2023/24 brightly, with four consecutive starts in league and cup competitions.

Ryan
ANDREWS
45

POSITION: Defender **COUNTRY:** England **DOB:** 26/08/2004

Young right-back Ryan Andrews burst on to the first-team scene towards the end of 2022/23, making his debut against Reading in the FA Cup that January before earning a first league appearance three months later. The Academy product - whose father Wayne also played for the Hornets - had featured seven times by the end of last term and he started 2023/24 brightly, making a first start in just the second league match of the campaign.

SQUAD
2023/24

James COLLINS 53

POSITION: Forward   **COUNTRY:** England   **DOB:** 31/12/2004

Teenage forward James Collins has impressed in the short time since his arrival from non-league Hertford Town in January 2023, notching a string of goals for both the Under-18 and Under-21 sides in the latter half of 2022/23. Following a bright start to 2023/24 - including scoring in the Under-21s' first league game of the season at Birmingham City - Collins was included in the senior squad for the first time for August's away trip to Stoke City.

Tobi ADEYEMO 54

POSITION: Forward   **COUNTRY:** England   **DOB:** 14/03/2005

Academy product Tobi Adeyemo lit up Vicarage Road with a memorable strike against Blackpool on his Championship debut in January 2023, just a week after his first senior appearance against Reading in the FA Cup. Having played five first-team games in all competitions - as well as making a valuable contribution to the Under-18s' run to the fifth round of the FA Youth Cup - Adeyemo was rewarded with a multi-year professional contract towards the end of 2022/23.

ONE OF THE HARDEST THINGS TO DO IN FOOTBALL IS TO STICK THE BALL IN THE BACK OF THE NET.

NOT LEAST BECAUSE THERE ARE USUALLY ELEVEN OTHER PLAYERS TRYING TO STOP YOU DOING JUST THAT!

SHOOTING FROM DISTANCE

Good service is obviously important, and a good understanding with your striking partner is also vital, but when it comes to spectacular strikes, practice is the key to hitting a consistently accurate and powerful shot and to developing the timing and power required.

EXERCISE

A small-sided pitch is set up with two 18-yard boxes put together, but the corners of the pitch are cut off as shown in the diagram. There are five players per team, including goalkeepers, but only one player is allowed in the opponent's half.

The aim of the drill is to work a shooting opportunity when you have the ball, with the likely chance being to shoot from outside your opponent's penalty area, from distance. The teams take it in turns to release the ball into play from their own 'keeper - usually by rolling out to an unmarked player.

18 YDS

KEY FACTORS

1. **Attitude to shooting - be positive, have a go!**
2. **Technique - use laces, hit through the ball.**
3. **Do not sacrifice accuracy for power.**
4. **Wide angle shooting - aim for the far post.**
5. **Always follow up for rebounds!**

SOCCER SKILLS

The size of the pitch can be reduced for younger players, and it should be noted that these junior players should also be practicing with a size 4 or even a size 3 ball, depending on their age.

WATFORD

11

ISMAËL
KONÉ

23

WATFORD WOMEN

2022/23 was an exciting season for Watford Women as they secured promotion back to the Women's Championship at the first time of asking.

They won the FA Women's National League Southern Premier Division with an impressive 53 points - the same tally as second-placed Ipswich Town, but the Golden Girls had a far superior goal difference.

Damon Lathrope's side won 17 of their league games, drew two and lost only three, scoring an impressive 65 goals in the process. There were high scoring home victories over Bridgwater United (5-1) and two 6-0 wins over Cheltenham Ladies and Crawley Wasps. On the road, Watford also put five past Milton Keynes Dons Women while keeping a clean sheet, and beat Plymouth Argyle Women 5-2.

Their league triumph set up a Championship play-off match against Northern Premier Division winners Nottingham Forest on May 23, 2023. Attacking midfielder Poppy Wilson's header proved the difference between the two sides as Watford triumphed, and that strike earned Wilson the Watford FC Women Goal of the Season award.

That victory made up for Watford's disappointment the previous month as Forest beat them 3-2 to lift the FA Women's National League Cup trophy. En route to the final, Lathrope's players saw off Norwich City Women 6-0 in the preliminary rounds before narrowly edging AFC Wimbledon Women 1-0 in the first round of the competition.

DAMON LATHROPE WAS NAMED THE SOUTHERN PREMIER DIVISION'S MANAGER OF THE YEAR AT THE 2022/23 FA WOMEN'S NATIONAL LEAGUE AWARDS.

The Golden Girls triumphed 5-3 over Hashtag United in round two, made light work of Milton Keynes Dons Women in the quarter-finals (5-1 win) and came out 2-0 victors over Wolverhampton Wanderers Women in the semi-finals.

In the Women's FA Cup, Watford thrashed Fulham 7-1 in the first round proper in November 2022, before putting six past Crawley Wasps with no reply in round two. Championship side Crystal Palace halted Watford's progress in round three as they were beaten 5-1 at Gander Green Lane.

In March 2023, Hornets legend Helen Ward announced her retirement from international football after scoring a record 44 goals in 102 appearances for Wales. On the same day, she also confirmed the 2022/23 campaign would be her last in the club game.

Ward spent two spells with Watford during her playing career, making her senior debut for the Golden Girls in 2001 before a 2009 move to Arsenal. She returned from Reading in 2017 and brought her goal tally for the club to 161 in her second spell in Hertfordshire. In August 2023, Watford FC Women confirmed Ward's appointment as General Manager.

WATFORD

DAZZLING
DEFENDERS

JOHN McCLELLAND, NIGEL GIBBS AND ROBERT PAGE WERE ALL GREAT HORNETS DEFENDERS. CONTINUING THAT PROUD TREND IS CURRENT WATFORD STAR RYAN PORTEOUS.

A true one-club man hailing from the local area, it's no wonder Vicarage Road fell in love with Nigel Gibbs.

Few, if any, supporters watching the bushy-haired, slight youngster make his debut in 1983 would have predicted he would still be there 19 years later, racking up just shy of 500 appearances over the course of a magnificent career in yellow.

A committed full-back, he made up for concerns about his small stature - Graham Taylor famously put him on a 'steak and Guinness' diet to 'beef him up!' - with dogged determination and an all-action defensive style. That's a surefire way to get the fans on side!

John McClelland's impact on Watford was felt so keenly, it was as if it represented a 'before and after' exercise. Prior to his arrival the team were conceding goal after goal, but once he was placed in the middle of the defensive line, the goals just ...stopped.

He was one of manager Graham Taylor's great finds. A player who was able to handle the strain that Watford's immense attacking emphasis placed on the defence. McClelland cut a mammoth figure at the back who also boasted a surprising burst of pace when needed.

His remarkable calm under pressure was regularly labelled his greatest attribute.

JOHN McCLELLAND

DATE OF BIRTH: December 7, 1955

PLACE OF BIRTH: Belfast, Northern Ireland

NATIONALITY: Northern Irish

WATFORD APPEARANCES: 234

WATFORD GOALS: 3

WATFORD DEBUT: November 10, 1984
Watford 3 Sunderland 1 (Division One)

NIGEL GIBBS

DATE OF BIRTH: November 20, 1965

PLACE OF BIRTH: St Albans, England

NATIONALITY: English

WATFORD APPEARANCES: 491

WATFORD GOALS: 7

WATFORD DEBUT: November 23, 1983
Watford 2 Sparta Prague 3 (UEFA Cup)

Born in Wales, but brought through the Watford academy, Hertfordshire was a home away from home for Robert Page as he enjoyed a superb eight years with the club.

He was given the honour of the captain's armband by manager Graham Taylor in 1997, paving the way for him to lead the Hornets out at Wembley in 1999, keep a clean sheet and secure the club's first-ever promotion to the Premier League.

Page led the defensive line with a bullish authority, going for every header, kicking every ball, and beating off any competition the manager signed for his position by upping his level again and again.

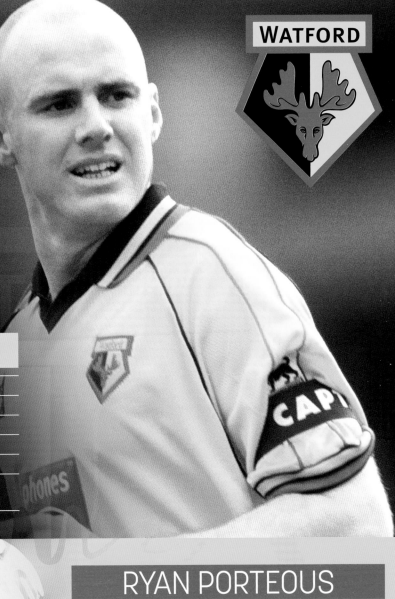

ROBERT PAGE

DATE OF BIRTH: September 3, 1974

PLACE OF BIRTH: Llwynypia, Wales

NATIONALITY: Welsh

WATFORD APPEARANCES: 252

WATFORD GOALS: 3

WATFORD DEBUT: October 16, 1993
Birmingham City 1 Watford 0 (Division One)

RYAN PORTEOUS

DATE OF BIRTH: March 25, 1999

PLACE OF BIRTH: Dalkeith, Scotland

NATIONALITY: Scottish

WATFORD APPEARANCES: 17*

WATFORD GOALS: 2*

WATFORD DEBUT: February 4, 2023
Reading 2-2 Watford (EFL Championship)

*AS AT THE END OF THE 2022/23 SEASON

Vicarage Road fell for Ryan Porteous pretty speedily; he's just one of those players fans warm to quickly, as his on-pitch demeanour is one of strength and leadership.

Signed only this year from Hibernian, the Scot has instantly installed himself as a key player in Watford's backline, with an old fashioned, no-nonsense defensive style plus great aerial ability, showcased perfectly by a goal on his debut at Reading.

He is the kind of presence who has future captain written all over him, and should his tenure with the Hornets extend to multiple years, no one would be surprised to see him wear the armband in a few years' time.

WATFORD

MATHEUS
MARTINS

FOOTY PHRASES

ALL OF THESE FOOTY PHRASES ARE HIDDEN IN THE GRID, EXCEPT FOR ONE ...BUT CAN YOU WORK OUT WHICH ONE? ANSWERS ON PAGE 62

WATFORD

```
C A E S W Y V V B H U G N U R Y M M U D
V U Q I D E R B Y D A Y O L U R T S S U
K F A D J L G T X T F C B E I A K C F P
I B H E O T L P Z R V N M W O J I R Y A
C M O F F S I D E R U L E E D S P E Y H
M E R U E I J R D E D A Q G S H L A X C
R X E R N H A T T R I C K O I L A M R T
E I Y O W S L S N O W R S O Z Y E Y A
D C A A Z L W S J K T K Y V K B M R T M
A A L P X A U Y H M I D F I E D A R O E
E N P T K N F W G C P L J K A M K N L H
H W E J A I L O K H A O F O H I E C G T
G A M E O F T W O H A L V E S T R N U F
N V A I A H E S L F J D U A O I U O T O
I E G B I C L A S S A C T U P F G E V N
V D G O A E E U C K S S C Y W U L Q L A
I R I R Q G M N S A C H G H D O S F G M
D V B A C K O F T H E N E T Z P X B N A
```

Back of the Net
Big Game Player
Brace
Class Act
Derby Day

Diving Header
Dugout
Dummy Run
Final Whistle
Game of Two Halves

Half Volley
Hat-trick
Keepie Uppie
Man of the Match
Mexican Wave

Offside Rule
One-touch
Playmaker
Scissor Kick
Screamer

PLAYER

OF THE SEASON

João Pedro ended his final season at Vicarage Road by landing the Graham Taylor Player of the Season award for 2022/23.

Voted the top performing Hornet last season by the club's supporters, the Brazilian forward netted eleven goals in 35 games for the Golden Boys as he pipped teammates Ken Sema (runner-up) and on-loan midfielder Hamza Choudhury (third place) to the prestigious award.

The 21-year-old set out his stall for the season with the only goal of the game to seal an opening-day victory over Sheffield United at The Vic. He further endeared himself to the Watford faithful with the third goal in our 4-0 mauling of local rivals Luton Town in October 2022.

Crucial braces then came in victories over Reading and Huddersfield Town before injury struck in December. João Pedro's absence from the team naturally left many wondering what might have been had he remained fit and available for the entire campaign.

Back in action in early February, João Pedro added three more league goals in the second half of the season to take his tally into double figures for the campaign.

Following the announcement of his move to Brighton & Hove Albion, the Hornets' final home game of the season provided João Pedro with the opportunity to say farewell to the Vicarage Road faithful while proudly collecting his Player of the Season accolade.

YOUNG PLAYER
OF THE SEASON

Full-back James Morris capped off an excellent season in Watford colours with the club's Young Player of the Season award for 2022/23.

Having made his Hornets' debut in the previous season's FA Cup tie with Leicester City, Morris enjoyed an extended run of first-team action last season and will be keen to cement a place in the Watford team during the current campaign.

Nominated for the award by the Academy leadership team of Richard Johnson and Jimmy Gilligan, left-back Morris featured in 14 fixtures in all competitions last season and saw his impressive contribution to the Hornets' cause rewarded with a new three-year contract at the end of the campaign.

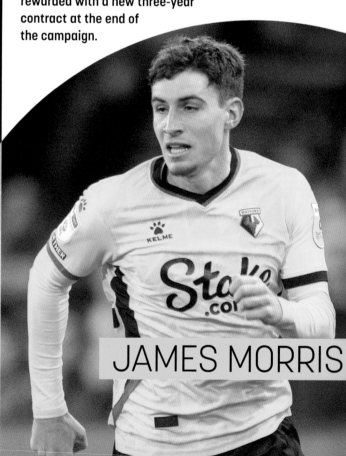

JAMES MORRIS

JOÃO PEDRO

THE WALL PASS

With teams being very organised in modern football, it can be very difficult to break them down and create scoring opportunities. One of the best ways to achieve this is by using the 'wall pass', otherwise known as the quick one-two.

EXERCISE

In a non-pressurised situation, involving four players, A carries the ball forward towards a static defender (in this case a cone) and before reaching the defender, plays the ball to B before running around the opposite side to receive the one-touch return pass. A then delivers the ball safely to C who then repeats the exercise returning the ball to D, and in this way the exercise continues. Eventually a defender can be used to make the exercise more challenging, with all players being rotated every few minutes.

The exercise can progress into a five-a-side game, the diagram below shows how additional players (W) on the touchline can be used as 'walls' with just one touch available to help the man in possession of the ball.

Each touchline player can move up and down the touchline, but not enter the pitch - they can also play for either team.

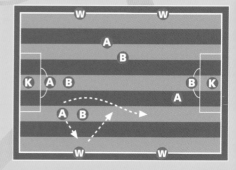

KEY FACTORS

1. **Look to commit the defender before passing - do not play the ball too early.**
2. **Pass the ball firmly and to feet.**
3. **Accelerate past defender after passing.**
4. **Receiver (B) make themselves available for the pass.**
5. **B delivers a return pass, weighted correctly, into space.**

SOCCER SKILLS

If done correctly, this is a tactic which is extremely difficult to stop, but needs teamwork and communication between the two attacking players.

WATFORD

FRANCISCO
SIERRALTA

3

A-Z

ARE YOU READY TO TACKLE OUR A-Z FOOTBALL QUIZ?

THE SIMPLE RULE IS THAT THE ANSWERS RUN THROUGH THE 26 LETTERS OF THE ALPHABET.

A
What nationality is Watford goalkeeper Daniel Bachmann?

A _____

B
Which team won the Sky Bet Championship title in 2022/23?

B _____

C
Which Premier League club reappointed their former manager as interim boss in March 2023?

C _____

D
Which League One side play their home matches at Pride Park?

D _____

E
What nationality is Liverpool's sensational striker Mohamed Salah?

E _____

F
Which country knocked England out of the FIFA World Cup finals in 2022?

F _____

G

Which famous football ground is due to host its final fixture in 2024?

G

H Which club did Neil Warnock lead to Championship survival in 2022/23?

H

I Which country did England defeat 6-2 in their opening game of the FIFA 2022 World Cup finals?

I

J Aston Villa winger Leon Bailey plays internationally for which country?

J

K What is the name of local rivals Luton Town's home ground?

K

L Can you name the League One club that play their home matches at Brisbane Road?

L

M Which Championship club boasted the division's top scorer in 2022/23?

M

ANSWERS ON PAGE 62

WATFORD

Q

Can you name the country that hosted the FIFA 2022 World Cup finals?

Q

R

Which Spanish side did Manchester City defeat in last season's UEFA Champions League semi-final?

R

S

Which team knocked Premier League champions Manchester City out of the Carabao Cup last season?

S

N

What nationality is Manchester City's ace marksman Erling Haaland?

N

T

Which full-back left Huddersfield Town to join Nottingham Forest ahead of their return to the Premier League in the summer of 2022?

T

O

Can you name the former Premier League team that will compete in the National League in 2023/24?

O

P

Which international striker ended five seasons with Norwich City in May 2023?

P

U

Can you name Brighton's German forward who joined the Seagulls in January 2022?

U

V

Can you name the former England striker who has hit over 100 Premier League goals for Leicester City?

V

W

What nationality is Ipswich Town's attacking midfielder Nathan Broadhead?

W

X

Can you recall the Christian name of the former Watford boss who took charge of Sheffield Wednesday in the summer of 2023?

X

Y

At which club did Leeds United's Luke Ayling make his league debut?

Y

Z

Which Dutch international midfielder played Premier League football for Chelsea, Middlesbrough and Liverpool in the 2000s?

Z

A-Z

PART TWO

ANSWERS ON PAGE 62

DESIGN A
FOOTY BOOT

WATFORD

Design a brilliant new footy boot for the Hornets' squad!

MIDFIELD MAESTROS

LES TAYLOR, JOHN BARNES AND TOMMY SMITH WERE ALL REAL CREATORS AND SCORERS IN THE HORNETS' MIDFIELD. CONTINUING THAT PROUD TREND IS CURRENT MAESTRO IMRÂN LOUZA.

John Barnes was plucked from relative obscurity at age 17 by legendary manager Graham Taylor, then thrown straight into senior football to help complete Watford's rapid rise from the fourth tier to the first.

His incredible, weaving dribbling style bamboozled defenders as he scored and created at will, entertaining Vicarage Road for six glorious years and representing Watford on the international stage with England. He would eventually go on to sign for Liverpool and win league and cup titles at Anfield.

Even to this day, there's a strong argument that Barnes remains Watford's most gifted ever player.

Les Taylor joined Watford as a winger, but by his own admission did not quite have the pace for the position. He was a steady enough presence from the flank in the early days, but it was when Graham Taylor converted him to central midfield that he really took off.

A master of setting the tone in the middle and breaking up attacks, Taylor's influence in midfield was felt keenly in every game. His leadership qualities were rewarded with the captain's armband and, in 1984, he led the Hornets out at Wembley for an FA Cup final.

LES TAYLOR

DATE OF BIRTH: December 4, 1956
PLACE OF BIRTH: North Shields, England
NATIONALITY: English
WATFORD APPEARANCES: 211
WATFORD GOALS: 20
WATFORD DEBUT: August 19, 1980
Luton Town 2 Watford 1 (Full Members Cup)

JOHN BARNES

DATE OF BIRTH: November 7, 1963
PLACE OF BIRTH: Kingston, Jamaica
NATIONALITY: English
WATFORD APPEARANCES: 296
WATFORD GOALS: 85
WATFORD DEBUT: September 5, 1981
Watford 1 Oldham Athletic 1 (Division Two)

An academy boy who rose through the ranks, scored some great goals and took in two separate spells with the club, it's no wonder Tommy Smith was (and remains) a firm fan favourite with the Vicarage Road faithful.

He hit his absolute peak in 2008/09, his final-ever season with Watford, incidentally, as he plundered 17 goals in the Championship playing in midfield.

The wing wizard boasted a wicked, whipped strike and an impressive poise on the ball, that paired with an unerring strike from twelve yards, formed the basis of an incredibly prolific 'goodbye' campaign for Smith.

TOMMY SMITH

DATE OF BIRTH: May 22, 1980

PLACE OF BIRTH: Hemel Hempstead, England

NATIONALITY: English

WATFORD APPEARANCES: 306

WATFORD GOALS: 64

WATFORD DEBUT: November 18, 1997
Watford 2 Oldham Athletic 1 (Division Two)

IMRÂN LOUZA

DATE OF BIRTH: May 1, 1999

PLACE OF BIRTH: Nantes, France

NATIONALITY: Moroccan

WATFORD APPEARANCES: 43*

WATFORD GOALS: 5*

WATFORD DEBUT: August 21, 2021
Brighton & Hove Albion 2 Watford 0 (Premier League)

*AS AT THE END OF THE 2022/23 SEASON

Every team needs an X-factor in midfield. In 2023/24, Imrân Louza is Watford's. Injury disrupted his 2022/23 season, but coming into this campaign fit and firing, there's hope and expectation that he can find his form and power the team to success.

He certainly has the tools to do it. His creative instincts have the potential to wreak havoc at Championship level, while his set-piece delivery is among the best in the division, providing constant danger.

He plays, passes and scores goals that will get Vicarage Road on its feet.

CLASSIC FAN'TASTIC

Harry the Hornet is hiding in the crowd in five different places as Watford fans celebrate promotion to the Premiership in 2006.

Can you find all five?

ANSWERS ON PAGE 62

WATFORD

TOM
DELE-BASHIRU

SCORES AFTER 33 SECONDS V QPR

24

WATFORD

GOAL
OF THE SEASON

This was a Watford goal that will be talked about for many years to come and was certainly an 'I was there' moment for the Watford fans that were in the stadium to witness it first-hand.

Despite this goal arriving so early in the season, it was always going to take something even more outrageous to prevent it from landing the title of Watford Goal of the Season for 2022/23.

Crowd favourite Ismaïla Sarr certainly provided Watford fans with many memorable moments across his four years at Vicarage Road and fittingly it was the Senegalese international who won the club's Goal of the Season award for 2022/23.

The campaign was just two games old when Sarr netted a spectacular David Beckham-style chip from inside his own half to put the Hornets in front away to West Bromwich Albion in August 2022.

In what was of course one of many 'Wow' moments from his Watford career, Sarr's goal at The Hawthorns opened the scoring after 12 minutes of frantic Championship action.

The 25-year-old forward took down a clearance before easing the ball out from under his feet and then sensationally sent a lobbed effort over stranded Albion 'keeper David Button from almost 60 yards.

ISMAÏLA SARR

V WEST BROMWICH ALBION

BEHIND THE

BADGE

...HIDDEN BEHIND OUR BEAUTIFUL BADGE?

WATFORD

A

WATFORD

WATFORD

WATFORD

B

C

48

F

WATFORD

G

WATFORD

D

WATFORD

E

H

WATFORD

8

JAKE
LIVERMORE

WATFORD

8

TRUE
COLOURS

HAVE FUN COLOURING
IN THIS PICTURE
OF HORNETS STAR
JAKE
LIVERMORE

STUNNING STRIKERS

ROSS JENKINS, LUTHER BLISSETT AND TROY DEENEY WERE ALL ACE MARKSMEN FOR THE HORNETS. LOOKING TO FOLLOW IN THEIR FOOTSTEPS IS CURRENT STRIKER MILETA RAJOVIĆ.

Luther Blissett is Watford's all-time appearance record holder and all-time record goalscorer. He enjoyed three separate spells with the club after graduating from the youth academy, cementing his status as a true homegrown hero.

He played a central part in the club's rise up the divisions in the late 1970s and early 80s, bagging goal after goal. A true poacher, always in the right place at the right time, he was particularly skilled in the air and scored a number of thumping headers.

Unsurprisingly, Blissett was the very first name voted into Watford's hall of fame, a just reward for his devotion over the years.

Towering target man Ross Jenkins was a big part, literally, of Watford's fairytale rise from the Fourth Division to the First in the late 1970s and early 80s.

Over the course of eleven years with the club he racked up 142 goals, making him the third-highest all-time goalscorer in Hornets history. Not only that, but he formed a fantastic bond with treasured hero Luther Blissett up front, playing in tandem with him and serving up chances where possible.

Jenkins showed impressive mental fortitude to put together such a career at Vicarage Road, having initially struggled to settle and score goals.

ROSS JENKINS

DATE OF BIRTH:	November 4, 1951
PLACE OF BIRTH:	Kensington, England
NATIONALITY:	English
WATFORD APPEARANCES:	398
WATFORD GOALS:	142
WATFORD DEBUT:	November 25, 1972
	Walsall 1-3 Watford (Division Three)

LUTHER BLISSETT

DATE OF BIRTH:	February 1, 1958
PLACE OF BIRTH:	Falmouth, Jamaica
NATIONALITY:	English
WATFORD APPEARANCES:	503
WATFORD GOALS:	186
WATFORD DEBUT:	April 3, 1976
	Watford 1 Barnsley 0 (Division Four)

Troy Deeney is responsible for one of the most iconic goals in English football history, turning a penalty for Leicester City into a goal for Watford in the 2013 Championship Play-Offs.

It's fitting that Deeney has a moment like this in the bank at a club he spent so long at, and did so much for.

He top-scored in seven of his eleven campaigns at Vicarage Road, led them to promotion in 2015 and helped establish the Hornets as a top-flight presence for the next half-decade.

His big, burly frame made him a handful for defenders, who could not cope with his aerial prowess and hold-up play.

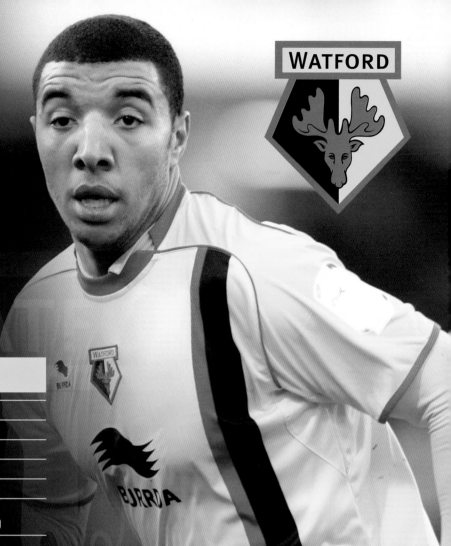

WATFORD

TROY DEENEY

DATE OF BIRTH: June 29, 1988

PLACE OF BIRTH: Birmingham, England

NATIONALITY: English

WATFORD APPEARANCES: 419

WATFORD GOALS: 140

WATFORD DEBUT: August 6, 2010
Norwich City 2-3 Watford (EFL Championship)

MILETA RAJOVIĆ

DATE OF BIRTH: July 17, 1999

PLACE OF BIRTH: Ballerup, Denmark

NATIONALITY: Danish

WATFORD APPEARANCES: 2*

WATFORD GOALS: 2*

WATFORD DEBUT: August 27, 2023
Watford 0-1 Blackburn Rovers (EFL Championship)

*AS OF SEPTEMBER 2, 2023

Mileta Rajović is the new No.9 at Vicarage Road, having joined from Kalmar FF in Sweden over the summer.

His goalscoring record in Scandinavia was very strong, and he got his Hornets career got off to a flying start, scoring twice on his first start in a pulsating 3-3 away draw at Coventry City.

Rajović is a towering presence at 6' 3", capable of providing a focal point in attack and bringing the wide forwards and midfield runners into play, making him an excellent fit for Valérien Ismaël's tactical style and potentially the final piece of the puzzle.

REWIND

Watford 4
Luton Town 0

SKY BET CHAMPIONSHIP · OCTOBER 23, 2022

Watford turned on the style to secure the local bragging rights with an emphatic derby-day victory over arch-rivals Luton Town in October 2022.

The home team wasted little time and opened the scoring after just three minutes when Keinan Davis twisted in mid-air to meet Hassane Kamara's cross and give the Hornets a dream start. William Troost-Ekong stabbed home the Hornets' second from close range on the stroke of half-time.

Second-half goals from João Pedro and Ismaïla Sarr gave Watford their biggest home derby win and matched the 4-0 victory at Kenilworth Road in October 1997.

Norwich City 0
Watford 1

SKY BET CHAMPIONSHIP · JANUARY 2, 2023

An injury-hit Watford side made a winning start to the calendar year of 2023 with a hard-fought victory away to Norwich City on January 2.

After suffering disappointing defeats to Millwall and Swansea City during the Christmas period, the Hornets showed great character to bounce back with this winning performance at Carrow Road. Against a managerless Norwich side, Watford soaked up a great deal of pressure from the home team, but always looked a threat on the break. Their efforts were rewarded four minutes from time when Vakoun Bayo slid home a breakaway chance to secure all three points.

Watford 3
West Bromwich Albion 2

SKY BET CHAMPIONSHIP · FEBRUARY 20, 2023

Ken Sema was Watford's two-goal hero as the Hornets edged a five-goal thriller with WBA at The Vic in February 2023.

Sema set the Golden Boys en route to victory when he fired home from close range after 23 minutes. The visitors levelled early in the second half before Ismaïla Sarr dispatched a neat first-time finish to restore the Watford advantage. The Baggies bounced back again and drew level through Jed Wallace on 71 minutes. However, the Hornets were not to be denied and bagged all three points thanks to Sema who slammed home the winner with twelve minutes remaining.

FAST FORWARD

Leicester City (HOME)

SKY BET CHAMPIONSHIP · FEBRUARY 10, 2024

Something of a surprise arrival in the Championship for 2023/24 following relegation, Leicester City will provide the Hornets' opposition on February 10 in what could well be one of our toughest assignments of the season on home soil.

Despite last season's disappointment, the Foxes have enjoyed the most successful period in the club's history in recent times with City crowned Premier League champions in 2016 and FA Cup winners in 2021. Under new head coach Enzo Maresca, Leicester will be among the favourites for an instant return to the Premier League in 2023/24. The Foxes' arrival at Vicarage Road will of course bring back memories of our sensational Play-Off semi-final victory in 2013.

Leeds United (HOME)

SKY BET CHAMPIONSHIP · MARCH 29, 2024

Watford begin the busy Easter period with a visit from Leeds United, another side that suffered relegation from the Premier League last season.

Leeds will certainly be strongly fancied to mount a serious bid for promotion back to the top-flight at the first time of asking. Now under the management of former Norwich City head coach Daniel Farke, the German won the Championship title twice with the Canaries and will be going in search of a hat-trick of second-tier crowns in 2023/24. After that challenging encounter with Leeds United on Good Friday, the Hornets' Easter holiday programme concludes with a trip to face WBA at the Hawthorns on Easter Monday.

Southampton (AWAY)

SKY BET CHAMPIONSHIP · APRIL 13, 2024

With the important month of April seeing the Championship season heading towards its climax, Watford head to the south coast for a vital meeting with Southampton.

Just like Leicester City and Leeds United, Southampton were also relegated from the Premier League in 2022/23 and are sure to provide a tough challenge for the Golden Boys when they travel to St Mary's Stadium on Saturday, April 13. The Saints are another club who made a managerial change in the summer of 2023 with former MK Dons and Swansea City head coach Russell Martin being the man appointed to spearhead the Saints' promotion ambitions for 2023/24.

BEING PREDICTABLE IS EASY IN FOOTBALL.

DOING THE UNEXPECTED IS A LOT MORE DIFFICULT.

TURNING
WITH
THE BALL

One of the biggest problems a defence can have to deal with is when a skilful player is prepared to turn with the ball and run at them, committing a key defender into making a challenge. Because football today is so fast and space so precious, this is becoming a rare skill.

EXERCISE 1

In an area 20m x 10m, A plays the ball into B who turns, and with two touches maximum plays the ball into C. C controls and reverses the process. After a few minutes the middleman is changed.

As you progress, a defender is brought in to oppose B, and is initially encouraged to play a 'passive' role. B has to turn and play the ball to C who is allowed to move along the baseline.

The type of turns can vary. Players should be encouraged to use the outside of the foot, inside of the foot, with feint and disguise to make space for the turn.

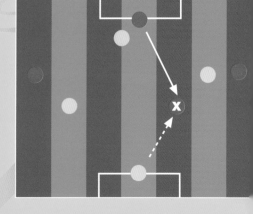

EXERCISE 2

As the players grow in confidence, you can move forward to a small-sided game. In this example of a 4-a-side practice match, X has made space for themselves to turn with the ball, by coming off the defender at an angle. By doing this X can see that the defender has not tracked them, and therefore has the awareness to turn and attack.

SOCCER
SKILLS

Matches at the top level are won and lost by pieces of skill such as this, so players have to be brave enough to go in search of the ball, and turn in tight situations.

WATFORD

KEN
SEMA

12

WATFORD

HIGH FIVES

TEST YOUR HORNETS KNOWLEDGE & MEMORY WITH OUR HIGH FIVES QUIZ

1. Across the previous five seasons, who have been Watford's leading league goalscorers?

1. _____
2. _____
3. _____
4. _____
5. _____

3. Prior to Valérien Ismaël, who were the club's last five permanent managers?

1. _____
2. _____
3. _____
4. _____
5. _____

2. Can you name the Hornets' last five FA Cup opponents ahead of the 2023/24 season?

1. _____
2. _____
3. _____
4. _____
5. _____

4. Prior to this season's match v Stevenage, name our last five EFL Cup opponents?

1. _____
2. _____
3. _____
4. _____
5. _____

5. Can you recall the Hornets' final league position from each of the last five seasons?

1. _____
2. _____
3. _____
4. _____
5. _____

6. Which members of the Watford squad started the most league games last season?

1. _____
2. _____
3. _____
4. _____
5. _____

7. Can you remember these players' squad numbers from the 2022/23 season?

1. Craig Cathcart _____
2. Yáser Asprilla _____
3. Wesley Hoedt _____
4. Ken Sema _____
5. Jeremy Ngakia _____

8. Can you recall the score and season from the last five derby wins over rivals Luton Town?

1. _____
2. _____
3. _____
4. _____
5. _____

9. Can you remember Watford's last five Championship victories from last season?

1. _____
2. _____
3. _____
4. _____
5. _____

10. Can you recall the club's final league points tally from the last five seasons?

1. _____
2. _____
3. _____
4. _____
5. _____

ANSWERS ON PAGE 62

SENSATIONAL STOPPERS

TONY COTON, ALEC CHAMBERLAIN AND HEURELHO GOMES WERE ALL GREAT HORNETS 'KEEPERS. CONTINUING THAT PROUD TREND IS CURRENT WATFORD STOPPER DANIEL BACHMANN.

It's not often a legendary career with a club starts at 32, but age proved no barrier to Alec Chamberlain, who spent just over a decade between the sticks for Watford after debuting in 1996.

Famous for his miraculous performance in the Play-Offs against Birmingham City in 1999, he made save after save and forced the game to a penalty shoot-out, where he then saved two spot-kicks en route to a win.

He stayed with the club during its ups and downs throughout the following years, eventually getting back into the top-tier and making a Premier League appearance in 2007, aged 42!

The undisputed greatest goalkeeper in Watford's history, Tony Coton is revered as a master of the craft up and down the nation.

The only player to win the Hornets' Player of the Season award three times, he was a telling presence between the sticks at a time where they badly needed one, as manager Graham Taylor's hyper-attacking approach regularly asked for heroics from those at the back.

Fans remember one performance in particular, a ten out of ten display away to Liverpool in the 1985/86 FA Cup quarter-final. His shaggy crop of hair and moustache became an iconic look during his time in Hertfordshire.

TONY COTON

DATE OF BIRTH: May 19, 1961

PLACE OF BIRTH: Tamworth, England

NATIONALITY: English

WATFORD APPEARANCES: 291

WATFORD DEBUT: September 29, 1984
Watford 4 Everton 5 (Division One)

ALEC CHAMBERLAIN

DATE OF BIRTH: June 20, 1964

PLACE OF BIRTH: March, England

NATIONALITY: English

WATFORD APPEARANCES: 287

WATFORD DEBUT: August 31, 1996
Crewe Alexandra 0 Watford 2 (Division Two)

Heurelho Gomes arrived in England to much fanfare in 2008 with Tottenham Hotspur, but it was with Watford, from 2014 to 2020, that he truly showed what he was capable of.

Gomes was a vital presence in the 2014/15 season, which saw the Hornets promoted to the Premier League. He impressed greatly over the coming years, notably saving two penalties in the same game against West Bromwich Albion in 2016 and going on to win Player of the Season.

The Brazilian truly embraced life in Watford both on and off the pitch, winning numerous accolades for his community work in the area.

HEURELHO GOMES

DATE OF BIRTH: February 15, 1981

PLACE OF BIRTH: João Pinheiro, Brazil

NATIONALITY: Brazilian

WATFORD APPEARANCES: 159

WATFORD DEBUT: August 9, 2014
Watford 3 Bolton Wanderers 0 (EFL Championship)

DANIEL BACHMANN

DATE OF BIRTH: July 9, 1994

PLACE OF BIRTH: Wiener Neustadt, Austria

NATIONALITY: Austrian

WATFORD APPEARANCES: 86*

WATFORD DEBUT: January 4, 2020
Watford 3 Tranmere Rovers 3 (FA Cup)

*AS AT THE END OF THE 2022/23 SEASON

Patience is a virtue for goalkeepers and Daniel Bachmann is proof of that. He joined Watford in 2017 and had to wait more than four years to make his Premier League bow, developing slowly and biding his time for his big chance.

He is now the undisputed first choice as the club look to get back to the Premier League, and recently signing a new contract affirms the new club captain's commitment to the Hornets' cause.

Bachmann's best trait is his shot-stopping. He kept 16 clean sheets despite a difficult 2022/23 campaign for the team, and he will be looking to improve on that this season in the Championship.

ANSWERS

PAGE 29: FOOTY PHRASES

Keepie Uppie.

PAGE 34: A-Z QUIZ

A. Austrian. B. Burnley. C. Crystal Palace. D. Derby County. E. Egyptian.
F. France. G. Goodison Park (Everton). H. Huddersfield Town. I. Iran.
J. Jamaica. K. Kenilworth Road. L. Leyton Orient. M. Middlesbrough
(Chuba Akpom). N. Norwegian. O. Oldham Athletic. P. Pukki, Teemu.
Q. Qatar. R. Real Madrid. S. Southampton. T. Toffolo, Harry. U. Undav,
Deniz. V. Vardy, Jamie. W. Welsh. X. Xisco Muñoz. Y. Yeovil Town.
Z. Zenden, Boudewijn.

PAGE 42: FAN'TASTIC

PAGE 48: BEHIND THE BADGE

A. Ryan Porteous. B. Francisco
Sierralta. C. Jeremy Ngakia.
D. Matheus Martins. E. Edo Kayembe.
F. Tom Dele-Bashiru. G. Jake
Livermore. H. Wesley Hoedt.

PAGE 58: HIGH FIVES

QUIZ 1: 1. 2022/23, João Pedro
(11 goals). 2. 2021/22, Emmanuel
Dennis (10 goals). 3. 2020/21,
Ismaïla Sarr (13 goals). 4. 2019/20,
Troy Deeney (10 goals). 5. 2018/19,
Gerard Deulofeu (10 goals).

QUIZ 2: 1. 2022/23, Reading
(third round). 2. 2021/22, Leicester City (third round).
3. 2020/21, Manchester United (third round). 4. 2019/20,
Tranmere Rovers (third round). 5. 2018/19, Manchester City (final).

QUIZ 3: 1. Chris Wilder. 2. Slaven Bilić. 3. Rob Edwards. 4. Roy Hodgson.
5. Claudio Ranieri.

QUIZ 4: 1. MK Dons (2022/23). 2. Stoke City (2021/22). 3. Newport
County (2020/21). 4. Oxford United (2020/21). 5. Everton (2019/20).

QUIZ 5: 1. 11th in Championship (2022/23). 2. 19th in Premier League
(2021/22). 3. 2nd in Championship (2020/21). 4. 19th in Premier League
(2019/20). 5. 11th in Premier League (2018/19).

QUIZ 6: 1. Daniel Bachmann (45 Championship starts). 2. Ken Sema,
Ismaïla Sarr & Hamza Choudhury (all had 36 Championship starts).
3. João Pedro (31 Championship starts). 4. Hassane Kamara
(30 Championship starts). 5. Keinan Davis (27 Championship starts).

QUIZ 7: 1. 15. 2. 18. 3. 44. 4. 12. 5. 2.

QUIZ 8: 1. 2022/23, Watford 4-0 Luton Town (Championship).
2. 2020/21, Watford 1-0 Luton Town (Championship).
3. 2005/06, Luton Town 1-2 Watford (Championship).
4. 1997/98, Luton Town 0-4 Watford (Division Two).
5. 1986/87, Watford 2-0 Luton Town (Division One).

QUIZ 9: 1. Watford 2-0 Stoke City. 2. Watford 2-0 Bristol City.
3. Watford 3-0 Birmingham City. 4. Watford 3-2 West Bromwich Albion.
5. Watford 2-0 Blackpool.

QUIZ 10: 1. 2022/23, 63 points. 2. 2021/22, 23 points.
3. 2020/21, 91 points. 4. 2019/20, 34 points. 5. 2018/19, 50 points.

CLASSIC FANTASTIC

Harry the Hornet is hiding
in the crowd in five different places
as Watford fans celebrate promotion
to the Premiership in 2006.

Can you find all five?